ANIMALS

Created by Claude Delafosse
and Gallimard Jeunesse
Illustrated by Tony Ross

A FIRST DISCOVERY **ART** BOOK

Cartwheel
·B·O·O·K·S· ®

SCHOLASTIC INC.
New York   Toronto   London   Auckland   Sydney

A cave in Lascaux, France

Artists have been painting animals for a very long time. Let's see what these early men are painting in a cave.

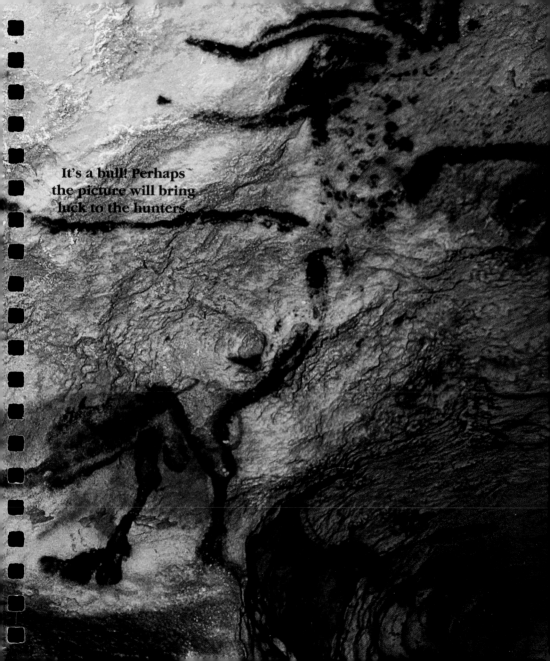

It's a bull! Perhaps the picture will bring luck to the hunters.

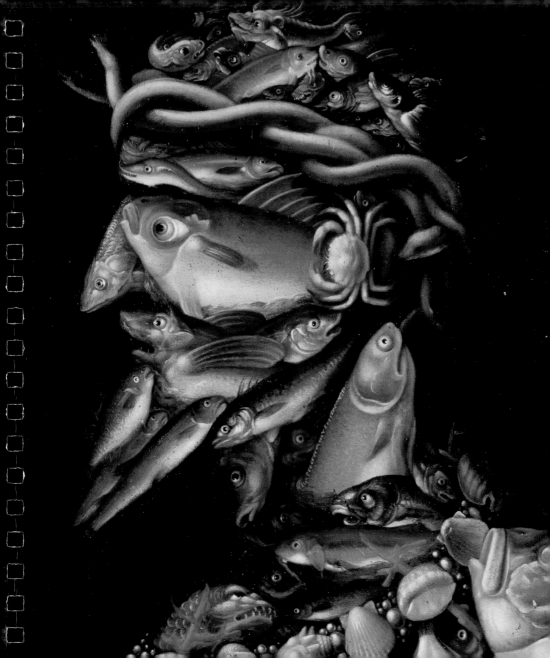

Would you like to see this pretty parrot go free? The door of the cage is open. Turn the transparent page to see what Cornelius Biltius actually painted.

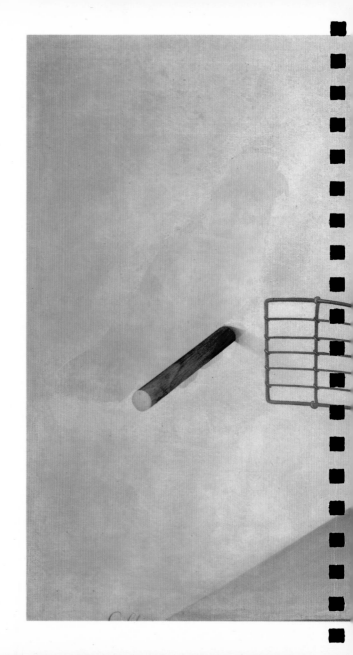

Alexander Calder used wire
to create this work of art.
It's a mobile—called *Fishbones*!

Henri Matisse used pieces of colored
paper to make the collage on the right.

Do you see why it is called *The Snail*?
Turn the transparent page to find out.

Does M.C. Escher's lithograph
look like a jumble of shapes?
See how the outline of one figure
helps to form the shapes of others.

Can you find an object here that is different
from all the others?
Now let's visit a gallery of animal paintings
and sculptures.

Two Monkeys
Brueghel the Elder

Do you see anything funny about some of the visitors to the gallery?

The Monkey Painter
Jean-Baptiste Chardin

Bastet Cat Lying with Its Kitten
Egypt

The Goldfish
Henri Matisse

The Cat
Alberto Giacometti

Statue of a
Buffalo, **China**

The Lady with the
Unicorn, **France**

Look closely at these details from the
works of art you have seen in this book.
Can you tell where they come from?

Why not make your own work of art?
Draw a picture or sculpt a clay model
of your favorite animal.

Table of Illustrations

Cover: **Henri Matisse**, *The Goldfish*, oil on canvas, 1912, Pushkin Museum, Moscow. Photo: Giraudon. © The Estate of H. Matisse.

Title page: **Alberto Giacometti**, *The Cat*, bronze, 1951, Berggruen Collection. Photo: Artephot/A. Held. © ADAGP, Paris, 1993.

Lascaux cave paintings, The Main Room, *Bulls* (detail), paint on rock, Superior Paleolithic (ca. 15,000 B.C.). Photo: Jean Vertut.

Giuseppe Arcimboldo, *The Woodsman*, oil on board, 1570, private collection. Photo: E. Lessing/Magnum. *Allegory of Water*, oil on board, date unknown. Collection Tappenbeck, Mauzay. Photo: Lauros-Giraudon.

Cornelius Biltius, *Parrot by Cage*, oil on canvas, ca. 1670, private collection. Photo: Bridgeman Art Library.

Alexander Calder, *Fishbones*, painted steel, 1939, The National Museum of Modern Art, Paris. © ADAGP, Paris, 1993.

Henri Matisse, *The Snail*, gouache on cut and pasted paper, 1953, The Tate Gallery, London. Photo and © The Estate of H. Matisse.

Maurits Cornelis Escher, *Mosaic II*, lithograph.© 1957, M. C. Escher Foundation, Baarn, The Netherlands.

Brueghel the Elder, *Two Monkeys*, oil on board, 1562, Gemäldegalerie Staatliche Museum, Berlin. Photo: J. P. Anders/BPK.

Jean-Baptiste Chardin, *The Monkey Painter*, oil on canvas, 1739–1740, Louvre Museum, Paris. Photo: RMN.

Egypt, *Bastet Cat Lying with Its Kitten*, stone, Low Epoch (1085–333 B.C.), Louvre Museum, Paris. Photo: RMN.

Mexico, *Toucan in Papier-mâché*, date unknown, private collection, Paris. Photo: Dagli Orti.

Henri Matisse, *The Goldfish*

Alberto Giacometti, *The Cat*

China, *Statue of a Buffalo*, porcelain, Tang Dynasty (618–907), Guimet Museum, Paris. Photo: RMN.

France, *The Lady With the Unicorn: Sight* (detail), textile, ca. 1500, Cluny Museum, Paris. Photo: RMN.

Other titles in the *First Discovery Art* series:
Portraits
Paintings
Landscapes

Library of Congress Cataloging-in-Publication Data available.
Originally published in France under the title *Le Bestiaire* by Editions Gallimard.

ISBN 0-590-55202-3

Copyright © 1993 by Editions Gallimard. This edition English translation by Jennifer Riggs.
This edition Expert Reader: Alice Schwarz, Museum Educator.

12 11 10 9 8 7 6 5 4 3 2 1   5 6 7 8 9/9 0/0

Printed in Italy by Editoriale Libraria

First Scholastic printing, October 1995